1 MONTH OF
FREE
READING

at

www.ForgottenBooks.com

By purchasing this book you are eligible for one month membership to ForgottenBooks.com, giving you unlimited access to our entire collection of over 1,000,000 titles via our web site and mobile apps.

To claim your free month visit:

www.forgottenbooks.com/free977463

ISBN 978-0-260-85900-6
PIBN 10977463

Our Motto : "THE WORLD FOR CHRIST"

(PROCEEDINGS)

MINUTES

OF THE

FORTY=FIFTH ANNUAL SESSION

OF THE

Trent River Oakey Grove Missionary Baptist Association

HELD WITH THE

Virgill Hill Missionary Baptist Church

Tuscarora, Craven County, N. C.

Rev. I. N. ELLIOTT, Pastor, Newbern, N. C.

October 18=21

1917

OFFICERS

Moderator, Rev. J. T. KERR, S. T. B., Jacksonville, N. C., P. O. Box 101.
Assistant Moderator, Rev. W. A. JONES, Maysville, N. C., R. F. D. No. 2, Box 4 B.
Clerk, HENRY J. HEMBY, Jacksonville, N. C., P. O. Box No. 32.
Assistant Clerk, L. R. REASE, Jacksonville, N. C.
Treasurer, GEO. WHITE, Jr., Jacksonville, N. C., R. F. D. No. 1.
Usher, Rev. WM. DOVE, Jacksonville, N. C.

Next Session will be held with Marshall Chapel Baptist Church, near Kellum, N. C., Onslow County.
Those attending Association will get off train at Kellum, N. C.

Improved Uniform Periodicals

FOR ALL GRADES

	In Quantities Per Quar.	Per Year	Single Copy Per Year
The Sunday School Worker	15 cents	60 cents	75 cents
Men's Class	12 cents	48 cents	60 cents
Home Department	8 cents	32 cents	40 cents
Adult Class	10 cents	40 cents	50 cents
Adult Class Teacher	15 cents	60 cents	75 cents
Young People's Class	10 cents	40 cents	50 cents
Young People's Teacher	15 cents	60 cents	75 cents
Intermediate Class	8 cents	32 cents	40 cents
Intermediate Teacher	15 cents	60 cents	75 cents
Junior Class	7 cents	28 cents	35 cents
Junior Teacher	12 cents	48 cents	60 cents
Primary Class	6 cents	24 cents	30 cents
Primary Teacher	12 cents	48 cents	60 cents
Bible Stories for Beginners	4 cents	16 cents	25 cents
Babyhood	3 cents	12 cents	20 cents
Picture Lessons	2½ cents	10 cents	14 cents
Bible Lesson Pictures	75 cents	$3.00	$3.00
Bible Lesson Leaflets	1½ cents	6 cents	10 cents
Junior Lesson Leaflets	1½ cents	6 cents	10 cents
Young People	17 cents	68 cents	75 cents
Girl's World	8 cents	32 cents	40 cents
Youth's World	8 cents	32 cents	40 cents
Junior World	8 cents	32 cents	40 cents
Our Little Ones	6 cents	24 cents	30 cents
The Young People's Service	6¼ cents	25 cents	40 cents

Sample Copies Free

AMERICAN BAPTIST PUBLICATION SOCIETY

1701-1703 CHESTNUT STREET, PHILADELPHIA, PA.

BOSTON: 16 Ashburton Place
CHICAGO: 125 N. Wabash Ave.
ST. LOUIS: 514 N. Grand Ave.

NEW YORK: 23 East 26th St.
LOS ANGELES: 313 W. Third St.
TORONTO: 223 Church St.

EXPLANATION.

_____

To the Members of the Trent River Association:—

Some, perhaps, have wondered why the Minutes are late in coming out, and, perhaps, thought the Secretary had not performed his duty, but this has not been the case. The main cause was in getting the covers from the American Baptist Publishing Society, owing to the hardships brought upon them by the selective draft law, in taking their trained men out of the office. Poor railroad transportation made them unable to deliver them to the printer until May 28th. The printer had the same hardships to undergo about obtaining help until, from the time the covers arrived, he was unable to get them out any earlier, owing to the condition of our country, brought on by the war. It has worked a hardship upon all industries. I trust that this may not happen again.

Wishing for a pleasant session at Marshall Chapel, I beg to remain,

Your humble servant,

H. J. HEMBY,
Secretary.

PROCEEDINGS

OF THE

Forty-Fifth Annual Session of the Trent River Oakey Grove Missionary Baptist Association, Held withthe Virgill Hill Missionary Baptist Church, Tuscarora, Craven County, N. C , October 18th to 21st, 1917.

At 10:30 A. M., Rev. J. T. Kerr, S. T. B., Moderator, called the Forty-fifth Annual Session of the Trent River Oakey Grove Missionary Baptist Association to order.

Praise services were conducted by Rev. L. L. Eadens, who lined Hymn No. 483, "How sweet the name of Jesus sounds," which was sung with much spiritual earnestness.

Scripture lesson was read by L. R. Rease from the 16th chapter of Proverbs. Rev. L. R. Rease offered prayer.

Rev. A. J. Jones sang a very appropriate hymn. Then the Moderator arose, in his usual dignified manner, and after making some brief, but timely, remarks, the house was announced ready for the dispatching of business. The Moderator before resuming his seat, brought forth a programme to be used as a guide in order to dispatch business in an easier manner, and, after a brief discussion, the same was adopted.

The Moderator called the pastor. Rev. I. N. Elliott, to come forth and deliver the welcoming address. The pastor arose, in his usual happy manner, and among the many good things, said as follows:

"Brother Moderator and Members of this Honorable Association:

"We have looked and anxiously waited for the arrival of this day, and the convening of this body.

"The day has come, and so have you. We have spared no pains, and left nothing undone that would prevent this from being one of the best sessions in the history of our Association. We welcome you to our homes, our church, and all of the rights that belong to Christians.

"We welcome you because we believe you are called of God to help organize the Christian forces and take the world for Christ. Never before has our love for the Saviour Jesus Christ been so highly exalted. Never before have we met so squarely at the altar of Christian fellowship. May the hallowed fire that shall be kindled here continue until every vestige of sin, ignorance and superstition shall be entirely obliterated from this fair land of ours.

"We welcome you one and all, as children of the Heavenly King, assembled here to further the mighty plan of salvation, and to consider how we can best promote the great principles upon which rest the foundation for the development of intellect and Christian welfare of the people of this country. By your assistance and co-operation we will be able to carry out the motto of Christ in every home. We invite you to our homes, trusting that you may reap as much benefit for yourselves as we anticipate by having you with us. We want you to stay with us, but if you have to leave, begin at once preparing to come again. Where you are welcome once, welcome twice, and always welcome."

Several of the members present stated that if words meant anything we were certainly welcome.

The welcome address and responses being over, the house settled down to dispatch business.

The names of delegates were enrolled, and the Moderator appointed the following committees, viz:

A committee of seven on Nominating Officers.

A committee of five on Special Sermons.

A committee of five on Temperance.

Committee of three on Printing Minutes.

Committee of three on Clerk's Services.

Committee of seven on Resolutions.

Committee of five on Finance.

Committee of five to select the Board of Directors for the Trent River Institute for the ensuing year.

At this juncture Rev. A. B. Vincent, of Raleigh, N. C.,

one of our State workers, had arrived. The usher brought him forward and introduced him to the Association. He spoke many timely remarks, and resumed his seat amid prolonged applause from the audience.

Rev. M. D. Stanford, of Wildwood, N. J., was next introduced. He made a brief talk, and spoke many words of truth.

Dinner now being ready, motion prevailed that we adjourn.

Doxology. Benediction by the Rev. A. J. Jones.

FIRST DAY—AFTERNOON SESSION.

The Association met pursuant to adjournment.

Praise services were conducted by Bro. J. C. Chadwick and Rev. S. L. Stanford. The 24th chapter of St. Matthew was read, and prayer was offered by Rev. S. L. Stanford. Rev. A. J. Jones sang an appropriate hymn, and the President, after making some timely remarks, announced the house ready for business.

Minutes of the forenoon session were read and approved.

Bro. W. M. Jones applied for membership in the Association. The Moderator appointed a committee to make proper investigation of the same and report its findings to the body.

The Moderator stated that according to the program the next in order would be the annual address.

The Moderator arose and delivered one of the most powerful addresses that has ever been delivered to any sitting of this Association. The speaker was frequently interrupted by applause.

On motion the annual address was ordered printed in full in the Minutes. (See address elsewhere.)

Dr. Vincent being present was introduced, and selected for his subject, "Why I am a Baptist." The subject was ably discussed. He gave many reasons as to why we are Baptists.

Revs. Lawson, Elliott, Jones and J. D. White spoke many words co-operating with Dr. Vincent.

Bro. Ed Mashburn, after making his report, was granted leave of absence for the balance of the session.

The Association adjourned, to meet again at 8 o'clock P. M. Doxology. Benediction by Rev. R. P. Lawson.

FIRST DAY—NIGHT SESSION.

The congregation reassembled pursuant to adjournment. The choir beautifully rendered, "Holy! Holy!" etc. Invocation by the Pastor, I. N. Elliott. Hymn by Rev. W. M. Dove, No. 378, "O for a Heart to Praise My God," etc., was sung with singleness of hearts. Rev. A. L. Miller read from the Book of Psalms, 122. Same offered prayer. Rev. N. A. Sandlin lined Hymn No. 434.

Rev. B. E. Davis arose, and making some preliminary remarks, delivered the introductory sermon from Rom. 58:35. Text: "Who shall separate us from the love of God?" The speaker held his own, and spoke many Gospel truths, and O, how our hearts did burn as he spoke, and we were made to feel it was good to have been there.

Revs. White and Kornegay lifted a collection of $8.00. Then Dr. Vincent made an appeal to the audience, and he received $1.50.

After making provisions for homes for visitors, the body stood adjourned, to meet at 9:30 A. M. Benediction by pastor.

SECOND DAY—MORNING SESSION.

The Association met pursuant to adjournment. Praise services were conducted by Bros. Walter Mack and C. D. Hatchel. Scripture lesson was read from the 24th chapter of Genesis. Prayer by Rev. J. D. White. Hymn No. 674, "O, for a Faith that Will Not Shrink," etc.

The Moderator, after making some very timely suggestions, announced the house was ready for the transaction of business.

The proceedings of the previous session were read and approved.

The roll of delegates was called, and the Committee on Nomination of Officers made their report. (See report elsewhere.)

Revs. A. J. Jones and J. D. White were chosen to escort the newly elected officers to their seats. Each of the officers arose and made short talks, thanking the Association for the honors conferred upon them, and promising to render at all times faithful services. The retiring officers made short talks expressing their approval of the selection of officers, and tendering many thanks for past honors, and pledging their unselfish support to this great cause.

All of the committees retired to get their reports ready to report to the Association.

A Committee on Devotional Exercises was chosen to arrange for preaching each day at the stand.

Committee on Printing Minutes reported. (See report.)

The Devotional Committee reported that Bros. Walter Mack. and H. L. Thompson would preach at the stand at 11:30.

The hour of 11:30 having arrived and, according to the programme adopted at the beginning of the Association, the regular routine business of the Association was suspended, and the following topic was discussed: 'How can we inspire greater interest among the churches to give more liberally for education?'

The discussion was ably led by Revs. J. D. White, T. Pearson and N. A. Sandlin. The speakers said, among the many good things, to inspire greater interest among the churches, conversion of heart, co-operation of pastors and their members, together with the influence and the hearty support of principal and officers of the school, would do more to espouse the cause of education, than anything else. The speeches were short, spicy and to the point, and full of good, wholesome advice.

Rev. M. D. Stanford, of Wildwood, N. J., being present, spoke many encouraging remarks upon the same subject.

The Moderator made some very timely suggestions, stating how money might be raised for education.

A motion prevailed to adjourn for dinner. Doxology. Benediction by Rev. M. Dillahunt.

SECOND DAY—AFTERNOON SESSION.

The Association reconvened according to adjournment. Rev. A. J Jones and Rev. S. L. Stanford conducted devotional exercises. Song No. 151 was lined and sung, then the Scripture lesson was read from the 15th chapter of St. John. Prayer was offered by Rev. S. N. Henderson. Then Rev. I N. Elliott led, "I'll Meet You in the City of the New Jerusalem,' etc., which was sung by the audience with much spiritual earnestness.

The Moderator announced the house ready for business. The proceedings of the previous session were read, and the names of delegates called. Same was adopted.

Rev S. Hill asked to be excused for balance of session, which was granted.

The Temperance Committee made its report. (See report.)

The Committee on Resolutions made their report. (See report.)

Bro. E. J. Hunter was excused to go home for balance of session.

The Committee on Clerk Service reported. (See report.)

Committee on Special Sermons reported. (See report.)

Bro. John Turnage was excused until tomorrow morning.

The amount of fifty cents was reported as collected from preaching held at the stand at 3 o'oclock.

The hour of 4:30 having arrived, the regular routine of business was discontinued for awhile, and the following subject was discussed by Revs. A. J. Jones and W. A. Jones "Duty of the Churches to the Association." The speakers made special emphasis of thorough organization of our Christian forces, to feel our brother's care; pay more money, do more Christian work, and champion and foster the cause of missions. Be loyal to the Association of which we are members, and as the delegates are the Church, then, when they, as a majority, meet in an annual body, it is our duty, as obedient citizens and Christian soldiers, to fall in line and obey the will of the majority, the great fundamental principle, which has had much to do in helping the grand old Baptist Church to attain its present success and usefulness. Many amens and applauses were heard among the congregation.

The body adjourned to meet at usual hour.

Doxology, Benediction by Moderator.

SECOND DAY—NIGHT SERVICES.

The congregation met according to adjournment. Praise service was conducted about thirty minutes before regular preaching hour. Services were conducted by Rev. M. Dillahunt and Rev. I. N. Elliott.

The hour having arrived for preaching, praise service was concluded. Rev. R. P. Lawson, who had been designated to preach the Educational Sermon, ascended the rostrum and, after making some remarks, he asked that Rev. M. D. Stanford, of Wildwood, N. J., be substituted in his place, which was accepted. Rev. Stanford arose and announced his text from the thirteenth Chapter of Corinthians, 12th verse. Among the many good things, the speaker said education helps us to see clearer, understand better, see things in a different manner than we did before being educated. He further stated that the foundation of education should commence in the home. The sermon was rich in thought, and contained many gospel truths, and was ably presented.

Rev. Elliott and his choir rendered most beautifully the sweet anthem of "I Can Hear My Saviour Calling," etc.

The Moderator made some timely remarks upon the same subject. Then Rev. J. E. Kornegay and Rev. M. D. Stanford came forward and lifted a collection of $16.05.

A letter from Dr. C. S. Brown was presented to the Clerk's desk, regretting his inability to attend the Association. He sent Miss Hallie H. Tucker, one of the State workers, and also agent of the Durham Reformer. The Moderator introduced her to the Association, and for thirty minutes she held the audience spellbound. The talk was one of the greatest appeals. After she concluded her address, a collection of $6.14 was given her for foreign missions.

Bro. John Dawson and Rev. N. A. Sandlin were excused for balance of term of Association.

After provisions for visitors and delegates, Association adjourned.

Doxology. Benediction by Rev. Elliott.

THIRD DAY—MORNING SESSION.

. The Association met according to adjournment. Praise services were conducted by Rev. W. M. Dove and L. L. Eadens. Hymn No. 293, "Father I Stretch My Hands to Thee," etc. Scripture lesson read from Romans 8:19. Prayer by Rev. L. L. Eadens. Hymn No. 492, "Amazing Grace,' etc   Prayer by Rev. R. P. Lawson.

The house was announced ready for business. The minutes of the previous session were read and approved. The names of delegates were called   The house settled down to business.   The following subject of "How Can We Stimulate a Greater Love and Pride for Our Denomination," by Revs. J. E. Kornegay and J. D. White. The speakers made special emphasis upon Baptist unity. Said they, "Let us all stand and work for one common cause   Let us stand upon the one true platform—one Lord, one Faith and one Baptism."

The committee selected to appoint the Board of Directors for the ensuing year reported. Their report was received and adopted.

The Educational Treasurer reported on hand $22.76.

The Moderator appointed three men to appoint an Executive Committee of seven for the ensuing year. Rev. Mr. Dillahunt came forward and briefly discussed the subject of "Why I Am a Baptist." He gave some very good reasons why he was a Baptist. The talk was timely, and enjoyed very much by all. Rev. A. L. Miller and Rev. R. P Lawson made some timely remarks upon the same subject. Rev. S. N Henderson gave some good thoughts upon the same subject.

The Committee on Finance reported.   (See report.)

Several of the churches failed to bring up as much money as the Constitution provides for, but the pastors promised to go back home and use all their influence to send up balance due.

The Secretary was ordered to hold over the minutes a reasonable time for the reception of said money.

Motion prevailed to adjourn for dinner. Doxology. Benediction by Rev. W. A. Jones.

THIRD DAY—AFTERNOON SESSION.

Met pursuant to adjournment. Praise service was conducted by Rev. A. L. Miller and Rev. M. Dillahunt. Hymn No. 490, "I Am Not Ashamed to Own My Lord," etc., was sung, after which a portion of the third chapter of Revelations was read as a Scripture lesson. Prayer was offered by P. H. Slade. Hymn No. 650, "The Church Has Waited Long," etc.

The Moderator announced the house ready for the transaction of business.

The minutes of the forenoon session were read, and the same were approved. The roll of delegates and ministers was called, and the Moderator designated the following to preach at the stand at 3 o'clock: Rev. A. L. Miller and Bro. L. M. Williams

The Executive Committee made its report. (See report)

Rev. J. T. Kerr was selected as a delegate to represent this Association to the Baptist State Convention.

Letters from St. John and White Oak were presented to the Clerks, asking for aid in erecting their churches. Each church was given $5.00 to aid them on their building.

On motion, we adjourned to meet again at Marshall Chapel, Kellum, Onslow County, N. C., commencing on Thursday morning at 11 o'clock before the third Sunday in October, 1918.

People attending this Association should get off the train at Kellum Station.

Members of the Association will be conveyed from the station to the church and back free of any expense.

Trains coming from Wilmington and Newbern Thursday and Friday and Saturday and Sunday will be met with conveyances to carry any one to church that desires to go.

For any further information concerning the sitting of the Association, or any available information desired, write H. J. Hemby, Secretary, Jacksonville, N. C., P. O. Box 32.

THIRD DAY—NIGHT SERVICES.

The congregation assembled before the hour of preaching had arrived, and praise service was conducted by Rev. A. J. Jones and L. M. Williams. Opening song No. 41. Scripture lesson read by L. M. Williams from the 95th division of the Psalms. Prayer was offered by Rev. T. Pearson. The choir rendered an appropriate hymn.

Then Rev. A. J. Jones, in a masterful way, introduced Rev. J. T. Kerr, S. T. B., to preach the Temperance Sermon. The speaker announced his text from the 24th chapter of Acts, 25th verse: "And as he reasoned Felix answered and trembled; go thy way; when I have a convenient season I will call for thee." The sermon was one of thought, sound in theology, plain and practical, and was delivered with power, and enjoyed by all who heard him.

Rev. A. J. Jones made some very timely remarks upon the sermon; then Rev. J. E. Kornegay and Rev. J. D. White came forward and lifted a collection of $7.65.

On motion of Rev I. N. Elliott a vote of thanks was tendered the people of the community for their kindness during the sitting of the Association.

SUNDAY MORNING SERVICE.

The hour having arrived for services, the congregation began to assemble, numbering at a close estimate 1,500 persons. The house was taxed to its full seating capacity, and many anxious hearers were on the outside seeking admittance. The choir opened the service by singing, "Holy ! Holy ! Holy !" Prayer by Rev. J. D. White. Hymn No. 480 was lined by Rev. R. P. Lawson. Prayer by Rev. A. L. Miller. Scripture lesson by Rev. R P. Lawson. The choir rendered a beautiful selection, then Rev. R. P. Lawson introduced Rev. T. Pearson, who was billed to preach the Doctrinal Sermon. Text from 2nd John 1–9 : "Whosoever transgresses," etc. Subject, "Obedience to the Lord." The sermon, upon a whole, was pronounced by those who heard it to have been a strong doctrinal sermon, such as the speaker always delivers when opportunity permits.

While the choir rendered many beautiful selections,

Rev. J. D. White and Rev. J. E. Kornegay came forward and lifted a collection of $24.21.

Doxology. Benediction by Rev. A. J. Jones.

SUNDAY EVENING 3 O'CLOCK SERVICE.

Praise service was conducted by Revs. W. M. Dove and L. L. Eadens. After praise service, the ministers spoke briefly upon the life and death of Rev. W. H. Haddock, of Pollocksville, N. C., lately deceased, and a member of this Association. The following ministers spoke upon his life and death : Revs. A. J. Jones, T. Pearson, R. P. Lawson and J. D. White. They said, in part, that his career as a citizen and a Christian was of the highest type, and worthy of commendation. Rev. White said the deceased asked him to sing the old favorite hymn of "When My Life Work Is Ended," etc., on his dying bed, which he did, and earth's loss was a Heavenly gain.

A collection of $3.05 was taken up and presented to the widows of the Scotts.

"Fight on My Soul 'Til Death," etc., was led by Rev. A. J. Jones, and sung by the congregation, with a parting handshake, hoping to meet again at Marshall Chapel.

The emerald forests, painted later in all the splendor of gayety have passed, and autumn, with its chilly winds, reminds us that winter is approaching. As we behold the field, which are brown, and the trees, whose leaves are falling, we are reminded of our own transit and sojourn on earth.

The Moderator having laid down his gavel, the Recording Secretary having stuck his pen away, and everybody is hurrying homeward, so I must bid you all au revoir.

REV. J. T. KERR, S. T. B.,
Moderator.

H. J. HEMBY,
Secretary.

COMMITTEE REPORTS.

COMMITTEE ON NOMINATING OFFICERS.

Brother Moderator:—We, your Committee on Nominating Officers, beg to submit the following report. After carefully considering the matter, we recommend that the following be elected as officers for the ensuing year:

Rev. J. T. Kerr, S. T. B., Moderator, Jacksonville, N. C.

Rev. W. A. Jones, Assistant Moderator, Maysville, Route No. 2, N. C.

Prof. H. J. Hemby, Secretary, Jacksonville, N. C.

Bro. L. R. Rease, Assistant Secretary, Jacksonville, N. C.

Bro. George White, Treasurer, Jacksonville, N. C.

Rev. W. M. Dove, Usher, Jacksonville, N. C.

H. J. HEMBY, Secretary,
REV. S. L. STANFORD, Chairman.

COMMITTEE ON SPECIAL SERMONS.

Brother Moderator:—We, your Committee on Special Sermons, beg to submit our report as follows:

Introductory Sermon, by Rev. S. N. Henderson.

Educational Sermon, by Rev. W. A. Jones.

Temperance Sermon, by Rev. L. L. Eadens.

Doctrinal Sermon, by Rev. J. E. Kornegay.

Missionary Sermon, by Rev. M. Dillahunt.

Respectfully submitted,

REV. J. E. KORNEGAY,
REV. L. L. EADENS,
REV. I. N. ELLIOTT,
H. L. THOMPSON,
REV. L. M. DILLAHUNT,
Committee.

COMMITTEE ON PRINTING MINUTES.

We, your Committee on Printing Minutes, beg to submit our report. We recommend that we have 1,200 copies of minutes printed.

PHILIP GOSS, Secretary,
N. L. KORNEGAY,
Committee.

COMMITTEE ON CLERK'S SALARY.

We, your Committee on Clerk's Salary, beg to submit our report. We recommend that we pay the Secretary, $20.00; Assistant Secretary, $3.50.

REV. A. J. JONES, Secretary,
REV. S. N. HENDERSON, Chairman,
N. A. SANDLIN,
Committee.

COMMITTEE ON RESOLUTIONS.

We, your Committee on Resolutions, beg to submit the follow-lowing report:

Section 1. This Association shall be divided into two Districts, No. 1 and No. 2.

Sec. 2. Resolved, That each church is to pay 5 cents per member each month that has five (5) Sundays; said money to be forwarded to the Union, wherever held in the District.

Sec. 3. Resolved, That there will be a meeting held in each District commencing on Friday before the 5th Sunday, at whatever place is chosen.

Sec. 4. All ministers and members are expected to give their support and encouragement in these meetings. Any minister or licentiate who wilfully absents himself from these meetings, personally or financially, will be subject to the Board, and each licentiate or said license will be revoked.

Sec. 5. Resolved, That each minister pay to these District Unions, 50 cents; Licentiates, 25 cents; Deacons, 20 cents; Laymen, 5 cents; said money to be forwarded to the District Union by messenger, pastor mail.

Sec. 6. Resolved, That each ordained Minister will pay yearly to the Association $2.00; Licentiates, $1.00; Deacons, 25 cents.

Monday after the fifth Sunday the chairmen of each District Meeting will meet at Jacksonville and make a report of the money collected for education.

Sec. 7. We recommend that this Association maintain a Ministerial and Deacon's Institute, conducted at some convenient place.

REV. J. E. KORNEGAY,
GEORGE WHITE,
REV. B. E. DAVIS,
BRO. L. R. REASE,
BRO. J. C. CHADWICK,
BRO. G. V. BROWN,
Committee.

COMMITTEE ON MODERATOR'S ADDRESS.

We, your Committee on Moderator's Address, beg to submit the following report: We recommend that the Annual Address be printed in full in the Minutes, and given the widest possible circulation. We further recommend that each Elder, Minister, Licentiate, Deacon and all members read it carefully.

REV. J. E. KORNEGAY, Chairman
L. M. WILLIAMS, Secretary.

REPORT OF EXECUTIVE COMMITTEE.

The Executive Committee took under consideration and performed the following work for the year:

The Board met Saturday and Sunday, May 12 and 13, 1917, and ordained two deacons and dedicated the church, Marshall Chapel. On May 21, 1917, the Board met at Pollocksville, N. C., at St. Phillip's Church, and considered the charge perferred against Rev. J. E. Kornegay for giving the Communion to members of the Belgrade Baptist Church which is not in fellowship of the faith. Rev. Kornegay acknowledged the charge. After some discussion the Board decided that he was guilty of vio.ating the law of the Church. Rev. Kornegay begged pardon, and he promised not to violate the law aga n knowingly. He was pardoned.

The second order in this meeting was to consider the case of Rev. B. E. Davis and wife. Both met the Board in this meeting, and made a full statemnt of the case. The matter had been in the courts at Newbern, N. C., and it was thought that if that evidence on which the decision was given, it might serve as evidence for the Board.

· The last work the Board did was at the Sunday School Convention that convened at the First Baptist Church, Jacksonville, N. C., in July, 1917. It considered the case of Rev. N. A. Sandlin, who was accused of giving open Communion to some of the members of old Town Creek Church, which church being not in fellowship with this Association.

Bro. Sandlin said he could not say that some had not taken with them at Mill Run, but it was not done intentionally. On Sunday morning of the Convention the Board took up the installation of the pastor of the First Baptist Church, in an impressive manner, Rev. J. T. Kerr as pastor.

REV. J. D. WHITE, Chairman,
REV. J. T. KERR, Secretary.

COMMITTEE ON TEMPERANCE.

Brother Moderator —We your Committee on Temperance, beg to submit our report

We hereby recommend that

Whereas, Intemperance is a growing evil, not easily put down, the use of intoxicants as a beverage is a moral blight and a social curse, and we recommend the language of St. Paul: "Now the works of the flesh are manifest, which are these: Adultery, fornication, uncleanness, idolatry, witchcraft, hatred, variance, emulation, wrath, strife, seditions, heresies, envyings, murderers, drunkenness, revellings and such like as I have told you before. But the fruit of the Spirit is love, joy, peace, long suffering, gentle, ness, goodness, faith, meekness, temperance; against such there is no law. If we live in the Spirit let us also walk in the Spirit." We further recommend that the pastors, in order to set good example, refrain from all strong drinks, the use of tobacco, and use all of the influence to save the men and women who will soon fill our places.

REV. J. D. WHITE, Chairman,
E. J. HUNTER, Secretary.

COMMITTEE ON MEETING OF NEXT ASSOCIATION.

The Committee on Meeting of Next Association beg to submit this report:

We recommend that the next Association convene at Marshall Chapel, Kellum, Onslow County, N. C., Thursday before the third Sunday in October, 1918, at 11:30 A. M.

H. J. HEMBY, Secretary.

FINANCE COMMITTEE.

We, the Finance Committee, beg to submit the following report:

We have carefully examined all letters that came to our hands, and we find them as follows:

Association Funds _____$ 98.04
Education Funds _____ 67.78

Total amount sent up _____$165.82

REV. S. L. STANFORD,
M. S. SHEPHERD,
WALTER MACK,
W. L. KORNEGAY,
——— Committee,

COMMITTEE ON DEVOTIONAL EXERCISES.

The Committee on Devotional Exercises beg to submit the following report:

Preaching each day at the stand at 11 and 3 o'clock.

WALTER MACK,
H. L. THOMPSON,
REV. I. N. ELLIOTT,
L. H. HURST,
W. M. WOOTEN,
——— Committee.

TREASURER'S REPORT.

Bro. Moderator:—I, your Treasurer, beg to submit this, my annual report:

Receipts—October 20, 1917.

From Rev. J. D. White _____$ 2.00
From Finance Committee _____148.38

Total received _____$150.38

Disbursements.

From October 20, 1917, to October, 1918.

To Secretary for Compiling Minutes _____$ 20.00
To Assistant Secretary for Services _____ 3.50
To the Moderator for Services _____ 2.50
To Vice-Moderator for Services _____ 2.50
To Treasurer for Services _____ 1.50
To State Convention fees to represent _____ 10.00
To Express on Minute Covers _____ 75
To Express on Minutes from Newbern to Jacksonville _____ 50
To Stationery _____ 30
To General miscellaneous expenses _____ 28.55
To St. John, for building expenses _____ 5.00
To White Oak, for building expenses _____ 5.00
To Rev. J T Kerr, for Traveling Expenses to State Convention _____ 14.05
To Jackson & Bell for Printing _____ 55.00
To Jacksonville Publishing Co., for Printing Programs _____ 2.50
To J. E. Dozier for oil at Association _____ 50

Total amount paid out _____$ 142.15
Total amount collected _____$ 148.38
Total amount of expenses _____$ 142.15

Balance on hand _____$ 6.23

GEO. WHITE, Treasurer.

ROLL OF DELEGATES.

N. T EVERETT,	MOSES JONES,
L. M. DILLAHUNT,	L. R. REASE,
N. L. KORNEGAY,	H. L. THOMPSON,
J. C. CHADWICK,	G. W. BROWN,
M. S. SHEPHERD,	HENRY BRYANT,
G. T. SHEPHERD,	L. H. HURST,
GEORGE WHITE,	J. T. TURNAGE.
CHARLEY GRIZZLE,	P. H. SLADE,
SIMOND LEARY,	JOHN DAWSON,
WALTER MACK,	OSCAR GREEN,
W. M. WOOTEN,	H. J. HEMBY,
R. KING,	P. G. GAUSE,
EUGENE WHITE,	E. J. HUNTER.

CHURCHES, CLERKS AND POSTOFFICES.

Oakey Grove—L. M. Williams, Route 2, Box 50_____Trenton, N. C.
Virgill Hill—F. T. Jeffres, R. F. D_____Clarks, N. C.
Sandy Run—George White, Route 1_____Jacksonville, N. C.
St. Phillip—Hasty Turnage_____Pollocksville, N. C.
Marshall Chapel—J. C. Chadwick, Route 2____Jacksonville, N. C.
Andrews Chapel—Oscar Green_____Holly Ridge, N. C.
Jenkins Chapel—R. H. Fair_____Sneads Ferry, N. C.
St. Louis—H. L. Thompson, Route 1_____Jacksonville, N. C.
David's Chapel—I. Scott_____Kuhns, N. C.
Hill's Chapel—Minnie Whitfield_____Trenton, N. C.
St. Marks—Benjamin Simmons_____Newbern, N. C.
Zion's Chapel—J. A. Wright, Route 1_____Pollocksville, N. C.
Evening View—Mrs. Ida B. Smith_____Jacksonville, N. C.
Oaks Chapel—Willie Murphy, Route 2_____Newbern, N. C.
Dixon Chapel—C. H. Shepherd, Route 1, Box 34_____Verona, N. C.
Henderson Chapel—Rachel Marshall_____Duck Creek, N. C.
Stockley's Chapel—Emma Moore_____Sloop Point, N. C.
White Oak—J. C. Wooten_____Maysville, N. C.
Mill Run—Calvin Boon, Route 1_____Verona, N. C.
First Baptist—Alice B. Kerr, P. O. Box 101_____Jacksonville, N. C.
Washington Chapel—Hattie Henderson
    Route 2, Box 45_____Hubert, N. C.
St. John—D. W. Jones, Route 2_____Maysville, N. C.
St. Stephen—Preston Ennett_____Silverdale, N. C.

EXECUTIVE COMMITTEE.

REV. J. D. WHITE, Chairman,	REV. J. T. KERR, Secretary,
REV. A. J. JONES,	REV. B. E. DAVIS,
REV. J. E. KORNEGAY,	REV. M. DILLAHUNT.
REV. W. A. JONES,	

OFFICERS OF THE ASSOCIATION.

Rev. J. T. Kerr, S. T. B., Moderator_____Jacksonville, N. C.
Rev. W. A. Jones, Vice-Moderator, Route 2_____Maysville, N. C.
Prof. H. J. Hemby, Clerk_____Jacksonville, N. C.
Bro. L. R. Rease, Assistant Clerk_____Jacksonville, N. C.
Bro. George White, Treasurer_____Jacksonville N. C.
Rev. W. M. Dove, Usher_____Jacksonville, N. C.

TIMES OF HOLDING QUARTERLY MEETINGS.

Rev. A. J. Jones, R. F. D. No. 2, Box 27, Jacksonville, N. C.
Oakey Grove—3rd Sunday in February, May, August. and
November.
Dixon Chapel—1st Sunday in March, June, September and
December.

Rev. J. T. Kerr, P. O. Box 101, Jacksonville, N. C.
First Baptist Church—1st Sunday in February, May, August
and November.

Rev. J. E. Kornegay, Trenton, N. C.
White Oak—4th Sunday in February, May, August and No-
vember.
Evening View—3rd Sunday in February, May, August and
November.
St. Louis—1st Sunday in January, April, July and October.

Rev. B. E. Davis, Newbern, N. C.
Sandy Run—4th Sunday in February, May, August and No-
vember.
Oaks Chapel—1st Sunday in March, June, September and
December.
Jenkins Chapel—4th Sunday in January, April, July and
October.
Henderson Church—3rd Sunday in March, June, September
and December.

Rev. J. D. White, 103 Main Street, Newbern, N. C.
Macedonia—3rd Sunday in March, June, September and
December.
Little Rock—1st Sunday in March, June, September and
December.

Rev. I. N. Elliott, Newbern, N. C.
Virgill Hill—2nd Sunday in February, May, August and November.
Andrew's Church—3rd Sunday in March, June, September
and December.
St. Mark—2nd Sunday in March, June, September and December.

Rev. N. A. Sandlin, Jacksonville, N. C.
Mill Run—3rd Sunday in March, June, September and De-
cember.
Washington—4th Sunday in February, May, August and No-
vember.
Zion's Church—1st Sunday in January, April, July and Oc-
tober.
Marshall Chapel—2nd Sunday in February, May, August and
November.

Rev. L. L. Eadens, Bayboro, N. C.
Stockley's Chapel—4th Sunday in March, June, Spetember
and December.

Rev. S. L. Stanford, Verona, N. C.

David's Chapel—2nd Sunday in February, May, August and November.

St. Stephen's—Letter did not state.

St. John—1st Sunday in March, June, September and December.

Rev. I. N. Elliott, Newbern, N. C.

Hill's Chapel—4th Sunday in February, May, August and November.

LIST OF ELDERS AND YEARLY FEES.

Rev. J. D. White, 103 Main Street, Newbern, N. C._____$2.00
Rev. S. Hill, Pollocksville, N. C._____ 2.00
Rev. T. Pearson, Jacksonville, N. C._____ 2.00
Rev. A. J. Jones, Route 2, Box 27, Jacksonville, N. C._____ 2.00
Rev. W. H. Moore, Newbern, N. C._____ 2.00
Rev. B. E. Davis, Newbern, N. C._____ 2.00
Rev. M. B. Bryant, Newbern, N. C._____ 2.00
Rev. J. E. Kornegay, Trenton, N. C._____ 2.00
Rev. I. N. Elliott, Newbern, N. C._____ 2.00
Rev. L. L. Eadens, Bayboro, N. C._____ 2.00
Rev. W. A. Jones, Maysville, N. C._____ 2.00
Rev. A. L. Miller, Newport, N. C._____ 2.00
Rev. S. N. Henderson, Jacksonville, N. C._____ 2.00
Rev. J. T. Kerr, Jacksonville, N. C._____ 2.00
Rev. N. A. Sandlin, Jacksonville, N. C._____ 2.00
Rev. R. P. Lawson, Snow Hill, N. C._____ 2.00
Rev. W. M. Dove, Jacksonville, N. C._____ 2.00
Rev. P. F. Murrill, Jacksonville, N. C._____ 2.00
Rev. I. P. Lovitt, Jacksonville, N. C._____ 2.00

LICENTIATE PREACHERS AND YEARLY FEES.

C. H. Smith_____$1.00
L. R. Rease_____ 1.00
L. M. Williams_____ 1.00
C. Mills_____ 1.00
M. L. Howard_____ 1.00
S. Marshall_____ 1.00
C. D. Hatchel_____ 1.00
Walter Mack_____ 1.00
E. T. Duncan_____$1.00
E. L. Washington_____ 1.00
T. B. Bryant_____ 1.00
H. L. Thompson_____ 1.00
D. Jackson_____ 1.00
Joseph Booth_____ 1.00
Oscar Dove_____
J. W. Koonce_____

LIST OF DEACONS AND YEARLY FEES.

G. W. Jones_____50c
W. M. Wooten_____75c
M. S. Shepherd_____50c
J. R. Shepherd_____
Luke Murphy_____50c
P. G. Gause_____50c
J. J. Sharpless_____50c
James Pollock_____50c
C. H. Mallett_____50c
B. R. Washington_____50c
Enoch Pearson_____50c
W. M. McAllister_____50c
W. H. Spencer_____50c
Eugene White_____50c
John Thomas_____50c
Joseph Arnold_____50c
E. J. Hunter_____50c
W. M. Anderson_____50c
J. E. Dozier_____50c
James Boyd_____50c
James Perry_____50c
W. H. Phillips_____50c
P. Bradley_____50c
E. W. Gillet_____50c
Frank Scott_____50c
Sam Strayhorn_____50c
P. H. Slade_____50c
W. L. Thompson_____50c
L. M. Dillahunt_____50c
A. P. Powell_____50c
R. King_____50c
I. J. Graham_____50c
John Scott_____
Henry Simmons_____50c
John Turnage_____50c
J. P. Phillips_____50c

OFFICERS OF THE NORMAL COLLEGIATE INDUSTRIAL TRAINING INSTITUTE, JACKSONVILLE, N. C.

Rev. J. E. Kornegay, President_____Trenton, N. C.
Rev. A. J. Jones, Vice-President, Route 2_____Jacksonville, N. Q.
Rev. J. D. White, 2nd Vice-President, 103 Main St____Newbern, N. C.
Rev. S. L. Stanfield, Treasurer_____Verona, N. C.
Prof. H. J. Hemby, Secretary_____Jacksonville, N. C.
L. R. Rease, Assistant Secretary_____Jacksonville, N. C.

FACULTY FOR 1917 AND 1918:

Prof. W. W. Parker, Principal_____Jacksonville, N. C.
Mrs. Maggie Cook, Assistant Teacher and
  Matron_____Jacksonville, N. C.

BOARD OF DIRECTORS FOR 1916 AND 1917:

Rev. J. E. Kornegay_____Trenton, N. C.
Rev. A. J. Jones, Route 2_____Jacksonville, N.
Rev. J. T. Kerr_____Jacksonville, N.
Rev. S. Hill_____Pollocksville, N.
Rev. W. A. Jones, Route 2_____Maysville, N.
Rev. J. D. White, 103 Main Street_____Newbern, N.
Rev. S. L. Stanford_____Verona, N.
Prof. H. J. Hemby_____Jacksonville, N.
George White, Route No. 1_____Jacksonville, N.
N. T. Everett_____Sneads Ferry, N.
E. T. Duncan, Route 2_____Maysville, N.
W. H. Phillips_____Jacksonville, N.
Rev. N. A. Sandlin_____Jacksonville, N.
Rev. W. M. Dove_____Jacksonville, N. C.

AUDITING COMMITTEE FOR 1917-1918:

REV. J. T. KERR,   REV. J. D. WHITE,
              GEORGE WHITE.

We, the Auditing Committee, beg to make this, our Annual Report:

We have carefully gone over the Principal's accounts, and according to his account, the Board owes W. W. Parker $787.94. To W. H. Phillips, $107.42 for services, work, supplies, etc., making a total indebtedness of $895.36.

                              REV. J. T. KERR,
                              GEORGE WHITE,
                              REV. J. D. WHITE,
                                        Committee.

PRESIDENTS FOR THE DISTRICT MEETINGS, 1918.

DISTRICT No. 1.

President, Rev. B. E. Davis; Vice-President, Rev. J. D. White.
Ministers in District—S. L. Stanford, N. A. Sandlin, A. L. Miller, I. P. Lovitt, S. Hill, Bros. L. R. Rease, C. Mills, M. L. Howard, O. B. Bell, J. W. Koonce, E. L. Washington, S. N. Henderson, W. M. Dove.

Churches in District—Jenkins Chapel, Henderson Chapel, Dixon Chapel, Andrews Chapel, Stockely Chapel, Mill Run, Washington Chapel, St. Louis, Union Chapel, Evening View.

DISTRICT No. 2.

President, Rev. A. J. Jones; Vice-President, Rev. I. N. Elliott.
Ministers and Licentiates.—T. Pearson, W. H. Moore, M. B. Bryant, J. E. Kornegay, W. H. Haddock, L. L. Eadens, J. T. Kerr, S. T. B., M. Dillihunt, R. P. Lawson, Bros. C. H. Smith, L. M. Williams, Walter Mack, E. T. Duncan, W. A. Hill.

Churches in District.—Oakey Grove, Sandy Run, Marshall Chapel, Virgil Hill, Zion Chapel, White Oak, First Baptist, Hill's Chapel, St. Phillip, David's Chapel, Oaks Chapel, St. John, Mt. Sinai, St. Stephen.

H. J. HEMBY, Secretary.

FOURTH ANNUAL CATALOGUE OF THE NORMAL INDUSTRIAL COLLEGIATE INSTITUTE, JACKSONVILLE, N. C.

SEVENTH SESSION—1916 AND 1917.

This attached form of catalogue gives sufficient information on course of study, expenses and regulations.

This School is under the auspices and supervision of the Trent River Oakey Grove Missionary Baptist Association.

LOCATION.—The School is situated on the west side of the Atlantic Coast Line Railroad, the only road between Newbern and

Wilmington. It is about one-half mile from the town of Jackson-ville, via Railroad, and one and a quarter miles to court house via county road. Geographically, the location is full of interest. The soil, a deep, sandy loam, produces potatoes, peanuts, cotton and corn in large quantities. It is favored with congenial winds and sparkling, pure water.

AIM.—The aim of the School is to teach young people to respect themselves and to respect others, as well, and to form correct habits of life; give them the proper mental discipline, that they will fit themselves to fill with honor the various positions of trust in the communities where they live.

Careful attention is given to the moral side of training. The School is not sectarian.

The School owns 3½ acres of land and three buildings. The main building is the school building, a large two-story building, with auditorium, recitation rooms and accommodation for twenty young men, a provision arranged for young men in the boarding department.

MEMBERSHIP.—All applicants for membership must have a good moral standing. Those from distances must furnish letters of recommendation.

RULES —Few rules, such as govern the best regulated homes, are given: 1. Neatness in dress and person; 2. Purity; 3. Clean-liness of desk, books and room; 4. Courteous to teachers and fellow students; 5. Punctuality in duty, earnest devotion to study, quietness in manner in all movements. 6. Obedience to law and duty.

LITERARY.—The students have exercise in reading, debating and orating as often as twice per month.

EXPENSES.—Tuition, according to grade, from 60c. to $1.50 per school month. Tuition and board, including lights and laun-dry for boys, $8.50 per school month; for girls, $7.50. Girls do their own work. Boys are to keep their rooms in good condition.

PRIVILEGES.—Students are expected to obey orders and rules of School. They are not allowed to leave School without proper permission. No visiting with local students. Students are expected to attend Sunday School and Church of their choice on Sunday at 11 A. M. and 2:30 P. M.

OUR NEEDS.—We need $1,000.00 to complete buildings and better equip our school; $600.00 to pay indebtedness.

We had 97 students in attendance last term. Three counties are represented.

DOMESTICS.—Sewing is the principal work under this head, Fancy work, Handycraft, Weaving and Crocheting are taught.

In sewing the different stitches, back stitching, button-holes and darning are given first attention. The other work comes in as occasion requires.

MUSIC.—Attention is given to Vocal music. Primary ideas are given special attention.

MISCELLANOUS.—Under this head house-keeping, community service, country life and sociology are taught.

The Visitations of officers, patrons and friends are appreciated and prove to be helpful to the School.

W. W PARKER, Principal,
Box 87, Jacksonville, N. C.

MRS. MAGGIE COOK,
Assistant Teacher and Matron,
Jacksonville, N. C.

STATISTICAL TABLE FOR THE YEAR 1917.

CHURCHES	Baptised.	By Experience.	Dismissed by Letter.	Excluded.	Deaths.	No. of Males.	No. of Females.	Total Membership.	Pastor's Salary.	Incidental Expenses.	Value Church Property.	Association Funds.	School Funds.	Balance Due.	Building Expenses.	Seating Capacity.	Sabbath of Meeting.	Received by Letter.	Restored.
Oakey Grove Chapel	5		1	1	1	33	81	114	$75.00	$3.00	$1,500	$11.40	$11.40		$150.00	400	3rd	2	4
Marshall Chapel	6	6		5	1	34	63	97	125.00	3.00	1,500	6.70	9.00	12.70		500	2n		8
Dixon Chapel	8		1	2	2	26	64	90	75.00	8.00	15.20	9.00	5.50	2.30	40.00	400	2		3
Sandy Run	7			5	1	26	52	78	175.00		3,000	7.80	1.10	9.40	2.30	300	1	2	2
Vgil Hill	2	4		5		34	67	101	120.00	5.00	1,600	9.70	2.50	5.80	135.00	500	4		2
Zion's Chapel	5					23	31	55	50.00		1,500	2.50	2.70		15.00	500	2		1
White Oak	6	2				15	12	27	100.00	3.00	8.00	2.70	6.18	10.45		200	1	3	1
Evening New	4	2	1	1	2	32	87	119	90.00		1,500	7.67	7.50		185.00	390	4		3
St. Louis	6	3				20	35	70	1,500	3.00	1,500	7.50	5.50			500	3		2
Hill's Chapel	2			1	1	9	11	55	115.00	2.00	9.50	5.50		73		500	1		2
Henderson Chapel				3		20	30	20			1,000	3.27	1.00	1.00	60.00				3
St. Philip	4	4						50	100.00	3.00	500.00	5.00	2.30		65.00	300	3	4	
St. Ak					2	5	8	13				2.30	1.00					1	1
Oaks Chapel	3	3				17	16	33	55.00			1.00	3.30	60		150	1		
Stockley's												3.30					3		
First Baptist Church	6	1			1	19	18	37	96.00	cents	2,000	1.50	3.50		2.20	500	1	1	1
Mill River	12	12		4		10	24	54	75.00	141.00	500.00	3.50		4.10	2.00	200	3	3	1
Washington	2	2		2		8	19	27	194.00	25.00	156.00	3.70	2.20	2.70	800.00	300	4	1	1
St. John Chapel	1	1			1	10	14	24	35.00	120.00	150.00	2.70	1.10		50.00	200	4	1	
St. Stephen's		2				5	6	11		2.00	200.00	2.20							
Davids Chapel	1					5	15	20	125.00		600.00	1.10	2.00			2500 200	2		3

Stockley's row: Paid one dollar and fifty cents — Rec eived no letter from church.

THE MODERATOR'S ANNUAL ADDRESS.

Delivered October 19, 1917, at Virgill Hill, Tuscarora, Craven County, North Carolina.

Brother Vice-President, Ministers, Delegates and Friends:

God, in His infinite wisdom and mercy, has permitted us to meet in this, the forty-fiith session of the Trent River Oakey Grove Missionary Baptist Association. Since we met last year, in this age of the highest Christian civilization known, blood has been shed in such a frightful and cruel manner that Christianity seems to veil her face in shame. The many battlefields that have been bathed in human blood call for serious cons deration. Christianity must yet unveil her face and strike the decisive blow before a complete victory is to be achieved. It does appear that Satan has risen to the highest power in Kaiserism to destroy men, women and innocent children. The Christian nations that stand for the protection of humanity must rise up and fight the foe until God gives a complete victory. But we must not lose our bearings in the midst of this great world-slaughter; we must not forget the great commission to go and make disciples of all the nations. When this has been complied with, the warring nations will throw down their swords and cry war no more. It is in obedience to this command that we are here today. We meet annually in one body to plan through prayer, praise and deep meditation how best we can carry out this great commission. And as we meet we should reaffirm our allegiance to the principles of the Baptist Church, as laid down in the New Testament by the Lord Jesus Christ. I am proud to be called a Missionary Baptist. I am satisfied with the principles of the Church, as laid down by Hiscox, which govern all Missionary Baptist churches in America and England, in other words, the whole denomination.

I can stand upon them with both feet. I don't have to straddle, and I don't like a straddler, because he is never safe. If you get at a straddler on one side, he dodges on the other side, and says it's in the Bible. But since we cannot be on every side, and we ought not to be so, let us stand firm in one doctrine, the doctrine of our Church. Let us be good Missionary Baptists, upholding the principles of that Church. I am proud of this mission field, which God permitted such pioneers as the Scots, and our own dear brethren A. J. Jones, Pearson and Moore and Henderson, to build and begin the great work to be carried on by their successors. These sainted pioneers built firmer than they knew. We thank God for their sons who have worked upon the foundation laid by these sainted pioneers. We believe in missions. When we speak of missions, we mean Home Missions, Education and Foreign Missions. I speak of the mission work in a three-fold point of view, because our Lord spoke of it from the same point of view. He spoke to His Disciples, and told them that they must be witnesses for me both in Jerusalem and all Judea, and in Samaria, and to the uttermost parts of the earth. Again he said unto them, "Go ye, therefore, and teach all nations, and make disciples of them." And again He said unto them, "Go ye into all the world and preach the Gospel to every creature." In every case he included everybody, and left none out. And one part is just as binding as the other.

You see, then, that those who insist in doing home missions and leave out foreign missions disarrange God's plan entirely, and arrange the whole matter to suit themselves. I declare unto you that God will reckon with these servants. We believe in Home

Missions, that the waste places may be built up, and the weak, struggling places may be strengthened and helped to get in position to support themselves. And that all the Christian societies controlled and operated, and all the agents and forces so adjusted to give the people more light of the Gospel of Christ. We also believe in education, and that all honorable efforts be made to educate the youth of our land, giving them the best moral, Christian and industrial training that it is possible to secure for them. We should give of the means that God has enabled us to get for the support of these causes. Wherever we can run and operate local institutions intelligently and free from the drudgery and unbearable strain where it exhausts every other line of work, we should support local institutions to better enable us to do the great work before us to grater advantage. These institutions should be managed and controlled by boards subject to the people, and who will adopt the best plans obtainable for the good of the work. The principles should be the best qualified men that can be secured, and who will make the work dear to his or her own self; make any sacrifice to bring success through the Spirit of Christ. In every case, these institutions should embrace territory enough to insure self-support to these schools, and when this can be done successfully they are to be and serve as feeders for the great Shaw University, where young men and women complete courses to fit them for life's arduous duty.

Foreign Missions.—I believe that it is just as obligatory to support Foreign Missions as Home Missions and Education. God's plan to save the world is by the preaching of the Gospel to all nations and peoples. So, then, it is divinely binding upon those who have the Gospel to give it to those who have it not. Africa, Hayti, China, India and the isles of the sea must have the Gospel if they are to be saved by God's means of grace. How are they to get it? It is your business who read these lines and hear me speak to help give it to them. If the gum-chewers sacrifice one stick a week for the work our board will be able to get the amount that it has pledged to give this year. Just as we have run away from God's plan of missions, we have run away from His plan in other things. God's plan, as expressed in the Bible, is for ministers and people to remain together as long as they can get along together. You cannot find any place in the Bible where it is intimated for the people to come together every year and elect a minister. He told them to go and preach, and when they fail to hear the message, go into another city. The present plan used by most of the churches is not God's plan, but man's plan. More evil comes from this manner of service than any other I know. When the end of the year draws nigh, and he does not know how he stands, his knees get weak, and he winks at many sins that he should strike square from the shoulder. If he has been faithful to condemn all sins and point them out, he will find that those whose toes have been mashed the most will set for him when election comes around. Why not come back to the Bible plan of doing business? There is among our ministerial brethren a great lack of Christian ministerial courtesy. So much so that if it is found out that a brother minister's time is about out, or if he has any dissatisfaction among his flock, another brother minister actually invades his brother's field, and gets another Sunday, and he actually goes in and begins to preach before the dissatisfaction is adjusted. This ought not to be so. If the ministers will not respect one another's rights, how can they expect other people to do so? One minister should not go into another brother minister's pulpit except through the invitation by the pastor. When the Lord unites a people and pastor the relation is too close to be thought of in such a trivial manner. He is the watchman of that people, the under shepherd, as long as he is pastor, and he is responsible for the instruction of that people to God. The deacon has not the right to ask another man to preach in his pastor's pulpit without permission from the pastor. I know some of you will say that that is a hard saying, but I am here to hold up the principles of the Baptist Church.

I believe that Baptists should read Baptist literature. As long as we pick up any kind of book because it looks pretty, we take it into our homes, and oft it turns out like taking a serpent into your bosom; It may remain quiet and may look pretty, but he is poison just the same. Bad literature turns out in the same way, however pretty it may be. It poisons the mind of the reader so much that he never again sees the right side of life. There should be a medium through which the presiding officer could speak to the people. Suppose all the churches recognized the Union Reformer; all he would have to do would be to write one letter to the Reformer, and you reading the Reformer would get it at once, instead of writing to every church or having bills struck to send to them.

RECOMMENDATIONS:

Since preaching a Gospel and leaving Foreign Missions out is a one-sided Gospel, I recommend that this Association give its hearty endorsement to Foreign Missions by giving an annual collection to the same. That we will bestir ourselves and keep the subject before the people and ask them to adopt the penny system recommended by the State Convention.

That we will instruct the people to use the Bible methods in calling pastors, and use the same method in separating the one from the other—the pastor and church.

That we ministers adhere more closely in recognizing the rights of a brother minister and in visiting the churches go the right way in—by the door.

That this Association recognize and patronize the Reformer published at Raleigh, for the interest of the Baptists of the State.

All of which we sincerely and humbly submit in this, our first annual address.

J. T. KERR,
Moderator

RULES OF ORDER.

----

1. On the meeting of the Association the President of the preceding session shall preside until his successor is made known. In case of his absence the Vice-President fills the seat.

2. Each session of the Association shall be opened and closed with prayer.

3. At each daily session the proceedings of the business session shall be read, and the names of the delegates shall be called; and no person speaking shall be interrupted until he is done speaking, unless he is out of order.

4. The members shall observe towards the officers and each other that courtesy that becomes Christians, and the person speaking shall in no wise reflect on the person who spoke before him, but shall express his idea.

5. Any member wishing to speak shall rise and address the President. He shall confine himself strictly to the subject under debate, and avoid all personalities.

6. No member shall speak more than twice on the same question without permission from the President.

7. All motions seconded shall be definitely stated by the President before discussion, and no brother shall be at liberty to whisper during the time another brother is speaking.

8. No motion shall be withdrawn after its discussion. The President shall not interrupt any member or prohibit his speaking, until he gives his idea on the subject, unless he violates the rules of the Association.

9. When a question is under discussion no motion or proposition shall be received except to adjourn, to lay on the table, to amend or postpone indefinitely, which several motions shall have preference in the order in which they are stated.

10. After a motion is decided, any member having voted in the majority, may move for a reconsideration.

11. No member shall absent himself during the session of the Association without permission of the President, and no one shall take final leave of absence without permission from the Association. If anyone shall do so, their absence shall be notied in the minutes.

12. All questions, except such as relate to the Constitution shall be decided by a majority of votes.

13. The Association shall have the right to decide what subject shall be admitted to its consideration.

14. These Rules of Order may be altered or amended at any session of the Association by a majority of votes.

RULES OF DECORUM FOR THE CHURCHES.

1. We will hold four council meetings in the year for the transaction of business; also special meetings whenever requisite.

2. The names of members shall be called at every regular meeting, and there shall be due notice taken of the absence of those who evince a disposition to absent themselves.

3. At every council, the pastor, in his right of office, shall preside as Moderator, and in case of his absence, the council shall appoint a Moderator pro-tem, who shall open the council with devotional exercises.

4. The Clerk shall keep a Church Book in which all the proceedings of the council shall be faithfully transcribed, and at every regular meeting the minutes of the preceding meeting shall be read immediately after the names are called.

5. An invitation shall be given to the brethren of our faith and order to sit with us in council, who shall enjoy all the privileges of the meeting, except that of voting.

6 Every subject for the consideration of the council shall be introduced by a motion which, when seconded, shall be debated and acted upon, unless withdrawn by the mover

7. Every speaker shall rise and address the Moderator by the appellation of brother, and continue his remarks to the subject under debate, and shall not be allowed to speak more than twice on one subject, except by permission of the Church.

8. No member shall withdraw from the council without permission from the Moderator.

9. It shall be required that in all matters of difference between members, before complaint is made to the Church, the aggrieved party shall have duly attended to the instruction of our Lord's Gospel recorded by St. Matthew, 11th chapter, 16th, 17th and 18th verses, and public offences, or such as operate against the peace of the Church, shall be the subject of discipline.

10. All questions submitted to the council shall be decided by a majority of votes, except receiving members to fellowship; and any question may be reconsidered upon the motion of anyone who voted in the affirmative.

11. The Moderator shall propound all questions for vote—shall keep the speaker to the subject under debate—may express his own views, after others are done speaking, and see that these rules are faithfully observed.

12. These Rules of Decorum may be altered or amended by a vote of two-thirds of the whole church.

Resolved, That this Council recommend the adoption of the foregoing Rules to all the churches that comprise this body.

CONSTITUTION.

Article 1. This Association shall be denominated and known as the Trent River Oakey Grove Missionary Baptist Association.

Art. 2. The object of the Association shall be the promotion of Christ's kingdom among men, and the means of accomplishing this shall be in strict conformity to the New Testament.

Art. 3. This Association shall be composed of pastors and delegates chosen by the churches connected with it, each church being entitled to three delegates.

Art. 4. The delegates from each church shall bear a letter certifying their appointment, and communicating information relating the state of the church.

Art. 5. The officers of this Association shall be a Moderator and Assistant Moderator, Clerk and Assistant Clerk, and Treasurer, who shall be annually chosen from among its members by ballot, a majority of its members voting, and continue in office until their successors are elected.

Art. 6. It shall be the duty of the Moderator to enforce an observance of the Constitution, preserve order, appoint committees, decide all questions, give his opinion on any question under discussion after others have spoken, and give the casting vote in case of a tie.

Art. 7. It shall be the duty of the Clerk to record the proceedings of each annual session, and to superintend the printing of the minutes and distribution of the same among the churches.

Art. 8. It shall be the duty of the Treasurer to receive all funds sent up by the churches or collected during the session of this body, and disburse the same as ordered by the Association. He shall make to the Association an annual report of the condition of the Treasury.

Art. 9. The Association shall appoint an Executive Committee, consisting of not less than five or more than seven members, which committee shall have the superintendence of Association missions and colportage. They shall have power to disburse all sums paid by the Treasurer of the Association for the objects under their charge, and during intervals between the meetings of this body, to receive and disburse funds for those objects, and to take such steps for their advancement as they shall deem advisable, and shall make an annual report to the Association of their doings.

Art. 10. This Association shall not maintain fellowship with any of her churches which neglect to preserve Gospel order.

Art. 11. This Association may invite visiting and corresponding brethren to seats, and extend to them all the privileges of the Association, except that of voting.

Art. 12. The annual session of this Association shall commence on Thursday before the third Lord's day in October, at such place as may be chosen.

Art. 13. By appointment of this Association, there shall be an Introductory Sermon of a denominational character, an Educational Sermon, a Temperance Sermon, a Missionary Sermon and a Doctrinal Sermon.

Art. 14. That we shall not receive any minister in our Association or pulpits until he has presented his credentials and recommendations from said church and Association from which he is a member of, and upon payment of $1.00 he may become a member of this Association. We will not fellowship any of our churches who receive any disorderly member from any of our churches within the bounds of this Association.

Art. 15. We recommend that none of our churches in this Association shall elect any minister as their pastor until he has presented his credentials and recommendations from his church and the Association which he is a member of.

Art. 16. Each church shall be represented by sending 20 cents to the Association, 10 cents for the Association and 10 cents or the Educational School Fund. This is to be paid by each member yearly.

Art. 17. This Constitution may be amended at any annual session by a two-thirds of the members present.

REV. J. T KERR, S. T. B., Moderator.

ORDER OF BUSINESS.

1. Enrollment of Delegates.
2. Organization.
3. Reception of Corresponding Delegates.
4. Appointment of Committees.
5. Call for Petitionary Letters.
6. Reading Church Letters.
7. Appointment of Corresponding Delegates.
8. Reports of Standing Committees.
9. Reports of Special Committees.
10. Report of Trustees of Ministers' Relief Society.
11. Report of Treasurer.
12. Motions and Resolutions.
13. Miscellaneous Business.
14. Adjournment.

BY-LAWS

OF THE

Trent River Oakey Grove Collegiate and Industrial Training School, Inc.

ARTICLE I.

Section 1. The membership of this corporation is composed of, and limited to the members of the Trent River Oakey Grove Missionary Baptist Association, which embraces the membership of the Missionary Baptist Churches (colored), of all of Onslow County, and a portion of Carteret, Craven, Jones and Pender Counties, except as hereinafter provided for.

All others wishing to become members may do so by paying an annual fee of One ($1.00) Dollar for each male and Fifty (50) cents for each female member, to become due on the 1st day of June of each year, and the membership of all such members shall terminate on the 1st day of July, unless renewed by paying the annual fee. Provided, however, that the Association by a majority vote may deny membership to anyone whenever they deem it to the best interest of this Corporation, or revoke the membership of anyone whenever they become detrimental to the purposes of this Corporation.

Sec. 2. The membership of this Corporation shall be represented in all membership meetings, by the Association, which is composed of the several pastors and three (3) delegates from each church or congregation, elected from the membership of said churches and congregations, within the bounds of the said Association.

Sec. 3. The annual meetings of the Association shall be held from Thursday to Saturday, inclusive, before the third (3rd) Sunday of October in each and every year at such place as may be chosen, when there shall be elected by a plurality vote, by ballot, fifteen (15) directors to serve one year and until their successors are elected and qualified. The pastors and delegates each shall have one vote on all questions except the election of directors, and then each shall have one vote each, for the full number of directors to be elected.

Sec. 4. Special meetings of the Association may be called by order of the Board of Directors, and it shall be their duty to call such meeting upon the written request of one-fifth of the representatives of the Association.

Sec. 5. A quorum shall consist of a majority of the representatives of the Association. If no quorum is present at any meeting it may be adjourned from time to time until a quorum shall be present.

Sec. 6. Two weeks notice of a special meeting of the Association shall be given to each representative personally, by mail to his last known address or by publication.

Sec. 7. The order of proceeding at all membership meetings in the Association for the purposes of this Corporation shall be as follows:

1st —Reading and approving minutes of former meeting.

2nd.—Report of Officers.

3rd.—Reports of Committees.

4th.—Reports of Board of Directors.

5th.—Report of Nominating Committee.

6th.—Election of Board of Directors.

7th.—Miscellaneous Business.

Sec. 8. The Association shall provide a committee of three members known as the Nomination Committee for the purpose of presenting names for election on the Board of Directors. Said committee to be appointed on motion carried, by the Moderator.

ARTICLE II.

Board of Directors.

Section 1. The affairs of the Corporation shall be managed by a Board of Directors, to consist of fifteen (15) members, to be elected annually, to serve for one year and until their successors are elected and qualified.

Sec. 2. The Board of Directors shall have the power to fill all vacancies in their body, from the representatives of the Association, until the next annual meeting of said representatives.

Sec. 3. The Directors shall have the power to elect or appoint all necessary officers and committees; to employ principals, professors, assistants and help of any and every class necessary for carrying out the purposes of the Corporation; to fix the amount of their compensation, to prescribe their duties; to dismiss any appointed officer, agent or employee without previous notice, and generally to control and manage the affairs of the Corporation.

Sec. 4. The Board of Directors shall meet at the same time and in the same place as the Association on Friday before the 3rd Sunday in October, of each year, and at the Union Meetings held in the interval between the annual meetings of the Association, in regular business meeting; and in special meeting at any time on the call of the President, and it shall be the duty of the President to call a special meeting, within ten days, upon the written request of one-third of the Board of Directors, which request shall state the purpose of the call.

Sec. 5. One week notice of special meetings of the Board of Directors shall be given by the secretary, to each Director personally, by mail to his last known address; and the purpose of the meeting must be stated in the notice of every special meeting; also the time and place of said special meeting.

Sec. 6. All special meetings of the Directors shall be held at the offices of the Corporation in Jacksonville, N. C., unless more convenient to meet elsewhere; when the President shall designate the place of the meeting in his call.

Sec. 7. A quorum shall consist of a majority of the Directors of the Corporation in all business meetings. If no quorum is present at any meeting it may be adjourned from time to time until a quorum shall be present.

Sec. 8. The order of proceeding at a regular meeting of the Board of Directors shall be as follows:

1st. —Roll Call.
2nd.—Reading and Approval of Minutes of Last Meeting.
3rd.—Reports from the Officers.
4th.—Reports from the Committees.
5th.—Filling Vacancies in Board of Directors.
6th.—Filling Vacancies of Officers.
7th.—Miscellaneous Business.

ARTICLE III.

Officers.

Section 1. The Board of Directors shall annually elect, at their regular meeting in October, the following officers, who shall hold their respective offices for one year, and until their successors are elected and qualified: A President, two Vice-Presidents, a Secretary and Treasurer.

Sec. 2. The Board of Directors shall fill all vacancies occurring among the officers.

Sec. 3. The Board of Directors shall confer on standing committees, hereinafter provided for, and any special committees they shall appoint, power to carry out the objects for which they are appointed.

Sec. 4. The Directors may, in the absence of any officer, delegate his power and duties to any other officer or to a Director, for the time being.

ARTICLE IV.

Duties of Officers.

Section 1. The President shall preside at all meetings of the Board of Directors; shall see that all orders and resolutions of the Board of Directors are carried out; appoint all members of committees not otherwise provided for; execute all conveyances, contracts and agreements, authorized by the Directors, either directly or upon the recommendation of committees, delegated with power to contract by the Board of Directors, and generally see that all the officers and agents of the Corporation perform their duties.

Sec. 2. The Vice-Presidents shall be the Chairmen and preside over their respective committees, as hereinafter described; and in the absence of the President they shall preside, in their order, at the business meetings of the Board of Directors, or attend to any of the duties as President they have the power to perform.

Sec. 3. The Secretary shall be the ex-officio Secretary of the Board of Directors, and keep the minutes of all proceedings in a book to be kept for that purpose. He shall be the Custodian of the Common Seal, and shall attest the same when affixed by order of the Board of Directors. He shall draw all orders on the Treasurer, and attest the same after being signed by the President and affix the Common Seal. He shall perform such other duties as the By-Laws enjoin, or is incident to his office.

Sec. 4. The Treasurer shall perform all the duties incident to his office, and usually performed by a Treasurer, and as such, he shall collect, receive and keep in safe deposit all the funds coming into his hands; endorse and collect checks and negotiable instruments, and keep full and accurate accounts of all receipts and disbursements; pay all orders signed by the President by authority of the Directors, and attested by the Secretary with the common seal affixed; rendering a full account of each regular Directors' meeting. At the expiration of his term of office he shall deliver to his successors all monies, books, papers and other property in his possession. The Treasurer shall enter into a good and sufficient bond in a sum in the discretion of the Directors conditioned on the faithful performance of his duties, and as security for all receipts coming into his hands. His books, records and accounts shall be open for inspection at all times to a committee hereinafter described, known as the Auditing Committee.

ARTICLE V.

Committees.

Section 1. The President shall appoint all members of committees, both standing and special, except as hereinafter provided, or unless otherwise ordered by the Board of Directors.

Sec. 2. There shall be a regular standing committee known as the Executive Committee, composed of five members, of which the first Vice-President shall be the Chairman. The duties of this Committee shall be to promote the objects of this Corporation by securing professors, teachers of ability, and seeing that every teacher, officer and employee does his full duty; to solicit aid for the Corporation from the various sources, keeping accurate accounts of all funds coming into their hands, which they shall turn over to the Treasurer, taking his receipt for same, and to have general supervision of all things necessary for carrying out the objects and purposes of this Corporation.

And to report of all proceedings to the Board of Directors, and the annual meeting of the Association.

Sec. 3. There shall be an Auditing Committee, composed of three members, of which the Second Vice-President shall be Chairman, the duty of which will be to audit all accounts of the Treasurer, members of the Executive Committee, and all other officers and agents of the Corporation of every kind who has any of the funds coming into their hands, and make their reports to the Board of Directors, and to the annual meeting of the Association.

ARTICLE VI.

Amendment of By-Laws.

Section 1. The Board of Directors of this Corporation shall have power, by vote of a majority of all the Directors, and without the assent or vote of the membership, through its representatives, to make, alter and amend the By-Laws of this Corporation, in meeting assembled, either regular or special, and if special, then the purpose of the meeting with the proposed amendments or alterations, must be stated in the call; but the By-Laws made by the Directors, under power, may be altered or repealed by the membership in regular meeting assembled.

CHURCH LETTER.

(Make out Letter carefully.)

_____191____

_____Chapel,

hereby makes the report for the year 191_____, as follows:

Baptised_____   _____

Restored_____   _____

Received by Letter_____   _____

By Experience_____   _____

Dismissed by Letter_____   _____

Excluded_____   _____

Deaths_____   _____

No. of Males_____   _____

No. of Females_____   _____

Total Members_____   _____

Pastor's Salary_____   _____

Incidental Expenses_____   _____

Value Church Property_____   _____

Association Fund_____   _____

Education School Fund_____   _____

Balance Due_____   _____

Building Expense_____   _____

Seating Capacity_____   _____

Sabbath of Meeting_____   _____

Owes now to Association_____   _____

Delegates_____

_____

Pastor in Charge_____

Church Clerk_____

Clerk's Postoffice_____

JACKSON & BELL CO., PRINTERS
WILMINGTON, N. C.
1918

The Scripture Readers' League

An organization to promote the reading of God's word among Men and Women, Young People, and Boys and Girls.

Membership in the League can be secured by writing the following application and sending for a copy of the Scripture Readers' League edition of the New Testament.

APPLICATION FOR MEMBERSHIP

I hereby apply for membership in the Scripture Readers' League. I enclose amount necessary for the purchase of the special edition of the New Testament. Please enroll my name and send me Certificate of Membership and button badge.

Signed...

On receipt of your pledge and amount for a copy of either edition of the New Testament a Certificate of Membership will be sent and a beautiful colored celluloid button without extra charge.

TESTAMENTS ARE AS FOLLOWS:

King James Version

STYLE No. 1—Clear, black-face type, self-pronouncing, bound in khaki Keratol, old color edge, limp, size of page, 4½ x 2⅝ inchesg Weight only 3 ounces. Price, **35 cents** net.

STYLE No. 2—Same as above. Bound in black Keratol, with overlapping covers. Price, **40 cents** net.

STYLE No. 3—Same as above. Bound in genuine French Morocco leather. Price, **50 cents** net.

STYLE No. 4—Same as above. Bound in genuine Morocco leather, **$1.00** net.

American Standard Version o the Scripture Readers' League New Testament.

Ruby type, self-pronouncing, size 2⅜ x 4 inches, only 5-16 of an inch thick, with the words of Christ printed in bold type. Printed on India paper.

S. R. L. No. 10—Khaki-colored linen, flexible covers, round corners, brown edges, gold back and side title, silk sewed, **35 cents** net.

S. R. L. No. 11—Black Keratol, cover overlapping edge, gold side title, red under gold edge, silk sewed, **50 cents**.

S. R. L. No. 12—Genuine leather, Morocco grain, flexible covers round corners, red under gold edges, gold back title, silk sewed, **90 cents** net.

AMERICAN BAPTIST PUBLICATION SOCIETY
PHILADELPHIA
Boston   Chicago   St. Louis   New York   Los Angeles   Toronto

KEYSTONE GRADED LESSONS
INTERNATIONAL COURSES

I. Beginners' Grade

TWO YEARS, COMPLETE

MARGARET COOTE BROWN

FOR TEACHERS

Beginners' Course. A teacher's illustrated text-book. **$1.00** a year. Quarterly parts, **25 cents.**

Beginners' Pictures. $3.00 a set for one year. **75 cents** for one quarter.

FOR PUPILS

Beginners' Stories. An illustrated paper for each Sunday. Single subscriptions, **40 cents** for one year. In quantities of five or more to one address, **7½ cents** each for one quarter; **30 cents** each for one year.

II. Primary Grade

THREE YEARS, COMPLETE

FIRST YEAR

ANTOINETTE ABERNETHY LAMOREAUX

SECOND YEAR

AUGUSTA WALDEN COMSTOCK

THIRD YEAR

ANNA EDITH MEYERS

FOR TEACHERS

Primary Course. A teacher's text-book. **$1.00** a year. Quarterly parts, **25 cents.**

Primary Pictures. $3.00 a set for one year. **75 cents** for one quarter.

FOR PUPILS

Primary Stories. An illustrated paper for each Sunday. Single subscriptions, **40 cents** for one year. In quantities of five or more to one address, **7½ cents** each for one quarter; **30 cents** each for one year.

III. Junior Grade

FOUR YEARS, COMPLETE

FIRST YEAR

HARRIET HILL

NEW EDITION, REVISED

SECOND, THIRD, AND FOURTH YEARS

AUGUSTA WALDEN COMSTOCK

FOR TEACHERS

Junior Course. A teacher's text-book. **$1.00** a year. Quarterly parts, **25 cents.**

FOR PUPILS

Junior Bible Work. In quarterly form, with suggestions for hand-work. Single subscriptions, **45 cents** for one year. In quantities of five or more, **9 cents** each for one quarter; **36 cents** each for one year.

IV. Intermediate Grade

FOUR YEARS, COMPLETE

REV. HERBERT FRANCIS EVANS

FOR TEACHERS

Intermediate Course. A teacher's text-book. **$1.00** a year. Quarterly parts, **25 cents.**

FOR PUPILS

Intermediate Studies. In quarterly form. Single subscriptions, **45 cents** for one year. In quantities of five or more to one address, **9 cents** each for one quarter; **36 cents** each for one year.

V. Senior Grade

FOUR YEARS, COMPLETE

FIRST AND SECOND YEARS

PHILIP A. NORDELL, D. D.

THIRD YEAR

O. P. EACHES, D. D.

FOURTH YEAR

PROF. E. B. POLLARD, D. D.

S. Z. BATTEN, D. D.

W. EDWARD RAFFETY, PH.D.

PROF. R. N. VAUGHAN, D. D.

A. H. NEWMAN, LL.D.

FOR TEACHERS

Senior Course. A teacher's text-book. **$1.00** a year. Quarterly parts, **25 cents.**

FOR PUPILS

Senior Studies. In quarterly form. Single subscriptions, **75 cents** for one year. In quantities of five or more to one address, **15 cents** each for one quarter; **60 cents** each for one year.

The prices given in this announcement include postage.

Sample lessons and full description will be sent free.

AMERICAN BAPTIST PUBLICATION SOCIETY

1701-1703 CHESTNUT STREET, PHILADELPHIA, PA.

BOSTON: 16 Ashburton Place.

CHICAGO: 125 North Wabash Ave.

ST. LOUIS: 514 North Grand Ave.

NEW YORK: 23 East Twenty-sixth St.

LOS ANGELES: 313 West Third St.

TORONTO: 223 Church St.

CPSIA information can be obtained
at www.ICGtesting.com
Printed in the USA
BVHW04*1221210918
528171BV00010B/490/P